Guthrie Clothing

The Poetry of Phil Hall

Guthrie Clothing

The Poetry of Phil Hall, a Selected Collage

with an
introduction by
rob mclennan

lps
LAURIER POETRY SERIES

WLU PRESS
WILFRID LAURIER
UNIVERSITY PRESS

Wilfrid Laurier University Press acknowledges the support of the Canada Council for the Arts for its publishing program. We acknowledge the financial support of the Government of Canada through the Canada Book Fund for our publishing activities. This work was supported by the Research Support Fund.

LAURIER Inspiring Lives. Canada Council for the Arts Conseil des Arts du Canada ONTARIO ARTS COUNCIL CONSEIL DES ARTS DE L'ONTARIO

Library and Archives Canada Cataloguing in Publication

Hall, Phil, 1953–
[Poems. Selections]
Guthrie clothing: the poetry of Phil Hall, a selected collage / Phil Hall; with an introduction by rob mclennan.

(Laurier poetry series)
Issued in print and electronic formats.
ISBN 978-1-77112-191-0 (paperback).—ISBN 978-1-77112-193-4 (epub).—
ISBN 978-1-77112-192-7 (pdf)

I. McLennan, Rob, 1970–, writer of introduction II. Title. III. Series: Laurier poetry series

PS8565.A449A6 2015 C811'.54 C2015-903248-2
C2015-903249-0

Front-cover image: Collage by Phil Hall made from torn-up scraps of the covers of his early books. Images on pages 55 and 56: Self-portraits by Phil Hall. Cover design and text design by P.J. Woodland.

Waterloo, Ontario, Canada
www.wlupress.wlu.ca

This book is printed on FSC® certified paper and is certified Ecologo. It contains post-consumer fibre, is processed chlorine free, and is manufactured using biogas energy.

Printed in Canada

FSC www.fsc.org RECYCLED Paper made from recycled material FSC® C103567

The failure of order is the work / disorder is not the work

—Phil Hall

Table of Contents

Foreword

Early in the twenty-first century, poetry in Canada—writing and publishing it, reading and thinking about it—finds itself in a strangely conflicted place. We have many strong poets continuing to produce exciting new work, and there is still a small audience for poetry; but increasingly, poetry is becoming a vulnerable art, for reasons that don't need to be rehearsed.

But there are things to be done: we need more real engagement with our poets. There needs to be more access to their work in more venues—in classrooms, in the public arena, in the media—and there need to be more, and more different kinds, of publications that make the wide range of our contemporary poetry more widely available.

The hope that animates this series from Wilfrid Laurier University Press is that these volumes help to create and sustain the larger readership that contemporary Canadian poetry so richly deserves. Like our fiction writers, our poets are much celebrated abroad; they should just as properly be better known at home.

Our idea is to ask a critic (sometimes himself a poet) to select thirty-five poems from across a poet's career; write an engaging, accessible introduction; and have the poet himself write an afterword. In this way, we think that the usual practice of teaching a poet through eight or twelve poems from an anthology is much improved upon; and readers in and out of classrooms will have more useful, engaging, and comprehensive introductions to a poet's work. Readers might also come to see more readily, we hope, the connections among, as well as the distances between, the life and the work.

It was the ending of an Al Purdy poem that gave Margaret Laurence the epigraph for *The Diviners*: "but they had their being once / and left a place to stand on." Our poets still do, and they are leaving many places to stand on. We hope that this series helps, variously, to show how and why this is so.

—*Neil Besner*
General Editor

Biographical Note

Phil Hall was born in 1953, and grew up in the countryside near Bobcaygeon, Ontario. He attended the last of the one-room rural schools, then Fenelon Falls High School, and in 1972 went to the University of Windsor, where he earned a B.A. and an M.A. and was mentored by Eugene McNamara, Alistair Macleod, and Joyce Carol Oates. His first book was published in 1973 in Mexico City. He began Flat Singles Press in 1976. In 1979 he moved to Vancouver, where he became associated with Tom Wayman and Erín Moure in the Vancouver Industrial Writers Union.

In 1985 he moved back to Ontario. In Toronto he taught at Ryerson and York universities, as well as Humber, Seneca, and George Brown colleges. Over twenty years he published six books of poetry with Brick Books. Notably, *Trouble Sleeping* (2000) was nominated for the Governor General's Award, and *An Oak Hunch* (2005) was nominated for the Griffin Poetry Prize. Hall has been in residency as a poet at the Pierre Berton House in Dawson City, Yukon; at Sage Hill Writing Experience in Saskatchewan; at the Banff Centre for the Arts; and at Queen's University, The University of Windsor, and the University of Ottawa.

In 2007 he and his wife, Ann, walked the Camino pilgrimage route to Santiago de Compostela in Spain. In 2011 his book of essay-poems, *Killdeer*, won the Governor General's Award for Poetry in English. This book also won Ontario's Trillium Award in 2012 and was nominated for the Griffin Poetry Prize. In 2012, at Queen's University, Hall set up and inaugurated an ongoing lecture series called The Page Lectures, in honour of Joanne Page. Each year, distinguished writers such as Stan Dragland and Elizabeth Hay are invited to speak.

As Poetry Editor at BookThug Press and as an editor/member of the Kingston Wired Writers group, Hall mentors new innovative voices. He is well known for his folksy yet challenging readings. Hall is a visual artist who works in assemblage. He plays clawhammer banjo and is a singer of old songs. He is devoted to the sequence poem and to small-press publishing. He lives near Perth, Ontario.

Introduction

Through the course of a career stretching back to the early 1970s, Canadian poet Phil Hall has become increasingly known as the "poet's poet," only becoming more widely known and appreciated during the past decade, with the publication of books such as *An Oak Hunch* (2005), *White Porcupine* (2007), *The Little Seamstress* (2010), his award-winning *Killdeer* (2011), and *The Small Nouns Crying Faith* (2013). With over a dozen books and chapbooks to his name, Hall has long been a poet of deep attention, compiling and collecting lines and phrases into an accumulation that speaks of small artifacts, and of a humanity rarely lived and articulated so well. His is a folk art, sketching out a collage of lines, phrases, and lost sentences. Stan Dragland, in *The Bricoleur and His Sentences* (Pedlar, 2014), refers to Hall as "the bricoleur's bricoleur," for creating his works out of the strands of what is available.

Hall's most recent half-dozen trade publications have clarified the collage aspect of his ongoing poetry and his adherence to the extended sequence. The poems offered here—as an alternative to a "Selected"—are a collage sampling of previously published lines, stanzas, and poem fragments worked and reworked, reshuffled and pared down, patterned by the poet into an entirely new structure. Nothing is fixed. Phil Hall's poems have become fluid, and refuse to remain static. This volume exists almost as a selected *poem*: one selected from the length and breadth of Hall's published work, from his early days in Windsor and Vancouver, through his stretch of years in Toronto, to his more recent years near Perth, Ontario, an hour's drive west of Ottawa.

Unlike poets such as Al Purdy and George Bowering, Phil Hall's work makes it impossible to excise any obvious series or sequence of "greatest hits"—i.e., poems that readers already know and love repackaged for the general reader. Instead, what becomes compelling about Hall's work is just how many permutations of this volume might have been possible, highlighting the remarkable durability of his writing. Hall's poems have the devastation of koans. He writes on influences, literary and otherwise; he writes of rural Ontario, attempting to speak of, and comprehend, a deeply personal family violence; he stitches together lines and tall tales and fables from his life—story shards from the ethos of his variety of Ontario wilds.

What remains curious is the length of time it took readers to catch up to his work. In *The Unsaid* (1992), he wrote "I am becoming more hermetic and more populist at the same time!" From the same collection, he referred to himself as "a Mandelstam in Guthrie clothing." He was writing out of labour songs and accidents, beauty and trauma. Yet his populist-leaning readers couldn't fathom his collaged use of language, prompting former "work poet" colleagues to respond with utter bafflement to a work that has since prompted comparisons and linkages to works by Don McKay and Erín Moure. Writing of Hall's linking of Osip Mandelstam to Woody Guthrie in *The Unsaid*, Ian Dempsey, in *cm*, writes "This schizophrenia is embarrassing at times in his poems, that is, it stops us from entering easily into his experiences. His poems lack the precision and grace of a classical expression, and only a few have the simple directness of popular pieces." It seemed as though those who were responding to his content didn't care for the language, and those who might have been attracted to his language weren't engaged with his content.

There is something of Hall's work that occupies a nebulous middle space amid polemics. As a poet he plays with experiment of sound and structure against a more traditional lyric and folk-narrative backdrop. Unfortunately, utilizing such a space between the two camps often leaves poets critically out in the cold. Other uncategorized Canadian writers might also include Erín Moure, Anne Carson, and Lisa Robertson, all of whom opened with a readership that didn't quite understand what they were doing but have managed to exist long enough to develop and to find their audiences.

Hall won the Governor General's Award for Poetry and the Trillium Award and was shortlisted for the Griffin Prize, for *Killdeer*, a collection that helped break through to a larger and long-deserved attention. Named for what had long become his token bird, *Killdeer* is a collection of self-described "essay-poems" published as part of BookThug's Department of Critical Thought. Writing on his token bird, Hall himself has discussed the deflections his work explores, attempting to distract you with one hand while performing some sleight unseen with the other. Unscathed, perhaps.

In an interview-review of *Killdeer* she conducted with J.A. Weingarten in *The Bull Calf*, Kait Pinder described the collection as "a commentary on and reconstruction of a tradition of lyric poetry in Canada in the twentieth century." She writes: "I see Hall describing lyric poetry itself as assuming the pose of the killdeer." Hall's early works included elements of work poetry, but he has morphed into a folk poet, composing what have evolved into "essay-poems." He practises a folk-local, examining the small and deeply specific, composing striking lines and phrases that accumulate into individual pieces, as well as sections of a far broader canvas.

At a reading in Ottawa in October 2014, Hall discussed the progression of his work, starting out as a true Ontario "son of Al Purdy," and deliberately working to evolve toward Louis Zukofsky's *80 Flowers* (1978), moving from anecdote and story to "that pure sound of the vowel." And yet his work encapsulates both equally, managing to evoke both a poetry constructed out of a striking play of language and also a core of human values and concerns. In his Afterword here, "To See It All & Not Be Weary," Hall articulates some of his argument against "fake innocence & irony."

Akin to the work of both Mandelstam (1891–1938) and Guthrie (1912–1967), Hall employs a distinct humanism, very much in the realm of "a philosophical and ethical stance that emphasizes the value and agency of human beings, individually and collectively, and generally prefers critical thinking and evidence (rationalism, empiricism) over established doctrine or faith (fideism)."[1] There's also an unabashed sincerity to Hall's poetry: one that cares enough to be both passionate and attentive at every turn; a poetry that deliberately disorients in order to reorient, presenting an entirely new way of seeing what we might already know.

Writing on *Amanuensis* for *Books in Canada*, Erín Moure described Hall as coming "by strife with words and their embedded values, to a technique of compression that reminds of Paul Celan's knotted poems; they beam straight through the skull." Writing on *An Oak Hunch* in *The Fiddlehead*, Ruth Roach Pierson referred to the "muscular musicality of the poems," just as Jamie Dopp wrote of *The Unsaid* a few years earlier in *The Malahat Review*: "The hermit impulse draws him to 'parsing, coining joint-words, genuflecting to Polish literature,' while the populist impulse has him 'pull[ing] on my slouch-cap … get[ting] out my songs, harmonica and confessions (confusions).'"

Genuflecting—as Dopp quotes him as doing—before those he admires, Hall picks up on deeds, words, and thoughts collected, considered, and absorbed. What is continually astounding about Hall's writing, working backward through his poetry collections, is the series of shifts, whether gradual or sudden, that bolt through. Move your way back from *The Small Nouns Crying Faith* to *Killdeer* and from *The Little Seamstress* to *White Porcupine* and you will begin to understand the differences in tone, mood, and question: urban explorations, questions of violence, and a dark rural history have shifted entirely to an ease and sense of peace in a country setting, sketching poems and fences and birds. His is a poetry that has moved from rage to joy, parsing history against a litany of events that have both shaped and scarred him. And yet his is a poetry in which the main goals might simply be, beyond attempting to write better, to understand exactly how to *be* better.

In his recent collections he has continued to explore and question through collaged fragments of turned and twisted phrases. Referencing Paul Celan, Hall combines words and the shape of sound to turn expectation. Hall is capable of switching as little as a letter or two in an expected word and then following the idea of that new word to almost illogical conclusions. Of course, the connection between Celan and Hall is far deeper than the twists of words; there is also an affinity with the ability to write beyond darkness, utilizing poetry to rebuild. Precision is an essential quality, even as Hall discusses in equal measure the impossibilities of such precision.

Hall's poems have evolved into explorations of the hows and whys of writing itself, and of how text is disseminated, articulated, generated. Hall is now allowing his pen a critical series of poetic breaths. The poems question, respond, reiterate, and shift, as the hand that scrapes the rural pen moves,[2] asking exactly what the meaning precisely means, and if meaning is even possible.

Somehow, his lines manage to self-contain so that even a shift in the order might still make the *selected collage* no less capable, and wise, as a reader familiar with his work might recognize a line or a fragment from his earlier books.

—rob mclennan

Notes

1. https://en.wikipedia.org/wiki/Humanism.
2. The title of Hall's 2013 chapbook is *A Rural Pen*, after a phrase by William Blake.

A Selected Collage

(bluegrass)

A man walks through half of the sun
over fallow land toward warm windows
each step he takes makes the earth boom
its guttural yodel in the old air

around him & outward in widening circles
animals scatter at breakneck & breakdown speed
their spasms of flight & of running
make the sound of hectic tin plinks

in the warm house a woman is red on one side
brown as bread on the other as her thoughts strum
over the fireplace & the humming children
over the vibrating blood of her husband's kill

near the garden the graves of their parents
lean together like a barber shop quartet
& the wind in the rotting tops of the carrots
releases their hopes in a lonely scraping of strings

✕

(for Men Against Rape)

A chainsaw is talking for the trees on the mountain
enraged   it empathizes   cries loudest   cannot believe

to listen to it   from down here   you would think it was a tree

or a god of witness   you would think no one was holding it
all morning the chainsaw's plea   *you will have to cut us all down*

✕

When I went down to the shore at dawn
to wash my facts & keep them green

war-torn decorum beads   hope-in-hell stones

the paedophile   my brother   had been there

again his fact   lay proven   *her loose fist*
at rest in the water   my facts bathe in

heart & anchor of my reflection

I look   so much like   my brother

×

My father said   *if you light that lamp*
I'll set your hair on fire   he set my uncle's hair on fire

when they were 3 & 6   my grandmother put out the hair

then beat my father   Cecil   with a razor-strop
she poisoned herself   that same year

but the lamp had been lit

~

Cec said   years later   the same thing again   to me

by telling me the story   & then   after I knew the story
real good   he could warn me   off   by only a look

at 60   I still see it   that look

~

I face   my father's contempt

because my grandmother beat him
& / or   because my uncle   *lit the lamp anyway*

not knowing what a symbol   of ardency   I would make of it

suicide   as always   has nothing   to do with anything
& no one cares   about my uncle   the hero here

ugly old   Uncle Elmer   who knit gloves

×

Though we all sink back together
for the same extra 5 minutes

our dreams eager to graze against us
uninfected by duty

soon we will rise
like fish to the sound of an aspirin

snowing loudly somewhere in the lake
near a hook with its barb filed off

×

The back townships acquiesce in the rain

Verulam   Somerville   Blythe

Devitt's Settlement   Lamb's School
Bury's Green

the stone-piles obscured in nets of downpour

each rock in a net-hole the water defines
as it filters around it to the ground

each rock hand-picked

in one farmhouse a child screams
at the rain because it will not stop

distinguishing his family from Noah's

screams   unchosen   at the chosen stones
no one will get through

till the rain halts
the net-strands fall away   are mud

the child listens to himself breath

he will never come back here
no matter what

✕

(guide to executive suicide)

Shoot yourself in the foot

Put your foot in your mouth

Put your money where your mouth is

Shoot your mouth off

✕

A chickadee
embeds itself
in the fog

watches
a crab-apple *sh*
a long time

puts its head
under its wing
to be more round

✕

I wanted to see a girl naked

so I tucked my genitals behind closed legs
only scant pubic hair visible

& balanced on a taped chair to see her torso
mine in the bathroom mirror

chiseled to sheer milk
tawdry

I wanted to be a goddess & a mortal mating

so I vanished into the Tommy Sweet tree
(from which Dad had hung the young wolf by its hind legs)

& there hidden by blossoms clung
pressing against apple wood until the sensation

from innocent hermaphroditics
self-loathing was born

the first mysogeny

×

(Bronwen Wallace)

She had the profile of a white owl sleeping
in an old Loyalist barn that had been converted
into a women's shelter

in my barn I am still being abused as a child
my glasses hurting my nose forced into the straw

but when she would pivot full-face toward me
& smile I saw what such barns as ours could house

now that she has darkened & flown
renovations are less possible

×

I worship our threatened complexity…want a flawed flow arbiters can't gussy…

Cacophony from the creaturely world goes into our speaking clearly

We write from within a reckless doubt that comes of carrying run-to-ground sorrow fervently as if it were the last live coal of this species

If I carry my sorrow-ember far and long enough it ceases to be my personal sorrow

Then from within its glow can be heard a cast of thousands enlisted from each station of the pecking orders: music not of sorrow but of spontaneous collective survival-fervor…

To smuggle language-jazz into amateur flatpicking ah-shucks confessionals: living on Foggy Mountain as we do, we'll use any animal in us to break it down

×

I am too old & no longer believe

a man should get down on all fours
& lick the rim of a woman's chamber pot

& beg to be led on a leash through the streets
naked   the way we used to

in Bruno Schulz's drawings
dwarfs on a pilgrimage to Distain

but once   loving a woman   too much
starved   scared   young
                                        & then when she was detained

I cut into wafers & ate her underthings

shoved my fingers down my throat
to hold her eaten underthings   in my hands again
& then swallow them again   like an ape

in Warsaw   skeletons were cutting green chunks
out of bombed horses in the streets at night

draping scraps in their pelvic bowls
                                                they'd run
& the meat would fall out
on dislodged cobbles

as they stooped
to grab back up their only meat
a puce heel-point might step on a hand-bone
                                                                        & laugh

so wasn't my depravity
at least the phlegm of a prayer   or an orchid of gesture

I swear I could see completely through her

at times she became a grenaded church window
& would let none of us hold her together

oh this one
she was as willfully ill-informed as D H Lawrence

humans once had the heads of birds   *or cats*
absolutely   she swore   *no question*

& the dead envy us our sleep   *don't try to deny it*

sleep is a luxury

no rest from facing it all at once forever
that's what death is

the doctor closes your eyes   *& they become lidless*

after I had ripped out the sunflowers
& smashed their faces against the fence

to my jealousy   she bellowed   *I loved them all*
& passed the bottle

her optimism had the rectitude of a martyr's stand-in

but I am too old   & no longer believe
she was even an ordinary window with smudges

I press my face against a clear ankle
watching yet for a sign of hope
                                        even in her disappearance

distain smoked & cured on the air

I contorting under safe-house pillows

no unbroken windows from those years

San Diego information
used to have a listing for one with the same name

& twice I left tears in a machine
                                         may it forgive me

some poor woman in San Diego
never answers
                      & this drunk accent keeps calling

she was old & my message came
without warning or mercy
                                   like the pogroms of our childhood

oh this one
she probably never anymore sets foot in the world

she & her cat   Undula   switch heads
                                             & laugh
as they replay me trying to tame our war

my liver no longer sings opera
my heart has foregone its tail

when quiet   sometimes   I hear you   Love

simply changing the pillow-cases
& humming our outlawed song

×

The tiny boat is slowing down
it doesn't want to get here

nor would I emulate classical tones
without smirking

×

To free me of anecdote

a woman whose friendship
could not over-ripen
by more than a drunken kiss
tasting of feta

a woman pivoting cameraward
on the Transcontinental

shouting Newlove from memory

waving Bliss Carmen's ring
at burning textbooks

she held the cork in the candle-flame
then drew Dali whiskers on me

forked me artichokes
fried in lemon juice with garlic
as good as ten mothers

posed with me with Santa
then sent me to Greece

history's blue oregano
indelible on me   thanks to her
faith in my male decency

& anecdote nothing

to live is to fly inside words
not stories or people

×

I couldn't write a better poem

because I needed a good grade
then I couldn't write an honest poem

because I wanted to get laid

then I couldn't write poems
that hadn't already been written

because it was my trade

I couldn't write a better poem
I was afraid

×

Spearing pineapple rings from a can with a stick

piqued by the moment's tenacity   in appreciation of
the wrecking yard around the epiphany

I have unfolded the road map of the ax-head
& found   even in its wagon ruts   & foot paths
the same devotion to flung balance   the same heirophany

a tree displays in its cold twigs   & seed tips
unfullbown   asymmetrical   ornament-hammered

gasket-crumbled   Father a serial killer of pets
Mother   a falsie shielding a prone *tick*

born joined at the head with myself   *monstre sacré*

hurt into balladeering   *take it away boys*   I have been verified
squat in song beneath the slide-rule bridge

darkness   yellow grass   a blip   gristle

Where wings once caught poor sinners like us
in billowing Tennysonian mounds

a tear has sprouted a white hair
as hard as a spike   but it will grow silky

if continents   again tonight   go to sleep turning pages

in a gathering flock that darkens the quiet
until each reader is the red-tailed hawk

on the fleur-de-lysed spire of the dance church

warily she hooks her beak into wet breast feathers
& lifts bifocals at a splinted angle   biting

we put on the hoods of our stories & fly inward

we pry open   & pick at   what nips the crux
of wings we don't have

while the wings we foreswear for sleep   shrivel   stink

& the ones we have turned our backs to in bed
are plucked awake at 5 a m to reinforce the moats

against the spike of the white hair piercing the tear

Do not tell me what is great
or how great gets made

tell me reknown has no split hoof
madness is privacy past its expiry date

tell me how the world can cripple
what should have been great-in-its-way

how form is the coward's defense against colour
beauty a roost

tell me how to bend lack
into a merit of language

a church & beans lingo
woven on surrural looms

don't show me how to growl & eat
coached eggs

×

(April 1970)

The day Celan saw Antschel in the Seine
& slipped into the ripples of the bookstalls

he rowed into the troughs of our shadows
into shadowed river bottom   into shadirt

he entered   *the round Zion of the water bead*
& the synagogue of the ear of corn

as Dylan Thomas showed us we could
into his mother's wide eye he returned   parsed

struck shine fading incredulous against mire
he sank through the curdled sheen of *Der Spiegel*

to smuggle labyrinthine green
back inside grey *Kampf*ortable tongues

his cemetery-lifeguard psalms sinking in us
yellowed scrap iron pleatings of despair

the same bookstalls   today   along the Seine
temple gardens shattered by his repair

grubbing   suckling   into these furrows
exhume die blessing-fossil

He was the skins of a few prides
each stuffed with shame

or the skins of a few shames
each stuffed with pride

if you figured out which
was the casing & which the filling

he'd change them around
& you'd get hurt

you'll get hurt   he'd warn
& look really hurt when he said it

×

There is a library of strangers in Dublin
Kraków Iqaluit Constantinople Petticoat Junction
I have borrowed two silences from—the best sleep of my life
& light moving in a Stan Brakhage film

far away at home at last
I could not be reached breached or dissuaded
I slept forever & took forever to wake up & when I did
there goes your mime teacher all in white

light was archeologizing a patchwork quilt on a bed
dusting each snag as if there were no budget constraints
the approach of the children & the long-eared goat
was a Latin declension enacted

there is a library of strangers in Dublin
the Troy-warrens of its archives boustrophedonic
silence stoops to eyeball each shard & tag it
light tests its white hands against walls in the air

(distracted indifference from the old goat & the children)

First   my first language   nonsense
over-hugged   my second language   sense

pre-morning fog   in the field-hollows
muffled the survey-quilts   & the deerstock

later   my first language   sense
dampered   my second language   nonsense

a quilt over green smoke smothered
the farmer-harlequin dubbed Quotidian

on the first day of deer season
away I rode a cock-hearse

was locked in the stocks of my name
in the public square

until an actual poem came
brandishing its turret-key   but no language

so I had to find one

×

Where #7's survey tangent
                                        cuts across the old lumber draw-roads
through limestone highlands   to the Ottawa

a starling picks at a blood-orange
thrown half-eaten to the gravel from a car ages away now

up close outcrops do-down pink & grey profiles in shadow

to the north   unclaimed swamps
                                        a broken throttled-smock blue

always about to get dark or rain   the blacks & greens
suspended   flinch   in a yellow-grey pectin

that is distance or history   *histance or distory*

indifference
that has never held a date or signature   nor will

only this relentless bifurcation

⁂

If I have to hear one more time
about the light from the star that's dead
or about the full moon's pull on a puddle
I'm going to shut down my observatory
& turn ruthlessly local

there's a look the elderly get
when they're eating soup   a reptile
focus   the tongue protrudes   the mouth puckers
& blows   it's disgusting   such devotion
but attractive too   because for that moment
the spoon is the moon

the idea dies
then the animal inside the idea
crawls out & clings

Me & Morrisseau were both abused as kids
both ran by rotgut then sang by hand
of a Canada that deplorably survives
high in the clawed glistening air

our giant muskrat soul kept falling apart
into butchered townships aflame with primal colour
& the spit of the grease was the shared song
of the brush & the pen slicing through forgiveness

✕

It is not you   it is the door   & then the phone
I open myself to cradle phonemes now that you are these things

~

My real feet in my knees
I kneel   to go with you

~

These binoculars
my handcuffs

×

People are like pens
in pens   they lie around for years
they never write anything

sometimes they dry up   so what
but mostly the ink is in there
dark & ready

wolves in marbles
foxfire hoof patents
etiquette muskies

×

My just-washed hair loosening & lightening in the wind

I walk down our deadfall path to Otty Lake my buckskin coat
the only sun

Two partridges wary stepping beak-regal pump rough
& fluster up thrown books fanning off into underbrush

The rain has ruined the purple mushrooms their black gill-feathers
are now a sticky guck

I am so gratefully dumb about "small lot management"

Our parents & the kids' pets are buried or scattered here
(along this lichened edge of Shield from Georgian Bay
to the Ottawa River)

I need socks oat cakes a hair-cut bug-spray

but my mind is on some young woman who glances back
over her shoulder past her bare & open ass with a look of
fear & resignation that should shame me but excites me

As a boy I was opened & hurt so I've always understood
if not shared a flinch of her degradation

But part of me is also an abuser who wants to *something*
so I don't have to be her

Instead   I pray   Conscience   Immune System
Earth's Atmosphere   Topsoil   the Periodic Table   bless us

She could be my daughter   18 next month   the creature
I love more than…

I'm 53   my Grey-Wing head   bowed   to mulch & kindling

When I walk back up the path   to our log cabins   a doe
is at the salt-lick   tick-bitten   scratched tame

We will watch each other   until guck   turns regal

Don't be discouraged by the prosaic origins of poems

Let the circus come to town   write it all out   the bearded
flashbacks   the two-headed incriminations

Let the stories set up their Big Top   let the barkers carney the rubes

Behind the trailers a giraffe is giving birth

Far from the roots of doors   their hands relaxed claws   the trapeze
family is snoring in harmony   what did you think the poem
was   join them

If you are lucky   when you wake up   this tent city will be a field
again   the circus will have pulled up & rolled away   your childhood
will have joined it

The newborn giraffe is in your arms   the ungainly   squirmy
actual   creature

Sing to it   to help it stand for the first time   like an unfolding
hinged ruler

In a memory of the creaking of ropes is the origin of a lullaby

Try again   devoid of guile or hoopla

×

What topsoil tells the hand   the hand tells a pencil
a pencil tells type   type tells a program   a program tells brains
brains tell the gods   & the gods tell topsoil:

feed the pinch or the swell

×

Boats revere words

poke the fish your eyeball with the tip
of a finger & push until the numb dot shows

oh sure some still hope to have less to do with necessity
& sentiment the further our expedition paddles into the
element-confusion of the ulterior but look along the far
horizon-edge New Sentences rear their grated feudalisms

water is stupid to trust us

prow row ow o

✕

A woman takes off her bombshell
& puts on her chicken   takes off her chicken
& puts on her bombshell   non-stop

as a man's swagger sags
to unveil his mother as an old man
in suspenders & mustachios

in a Booth Tarkington farce
at a local theatre when he was a boy
& didn't recognize his own mother

then did   halfway through
& had to be taken out   screaming
or are we talking two women here

or are we talking two men
either way   silent   a baby grand
in a shut-down woolen mill   high-strung

above a waterfall
at midnight   a waterfall
an infidel in a crinoline

×

(James Reaney)

Little Olson   that drunken blowhard
really laid it down solid a time or two   kingfishers & satyr-bikers
flung from a prolonged   sloppy   *Timber!*

meanwhile   our local giant
his marionettes enacting the Orange wars

his happy chicken harnessed to a carriage

& all three rings of his barn circus spinning windfall spokes
unbeknownst   in of all places London Ontario

where Whitman came to discuss cosmic consciousness
with Richard Maurice Bucke MD

where Greg Curnoe rode his paintings on glass around town

where journaling Roy McDonald abides…

Olson & Whitman   *the Push & the Yawp*
amount to not much around here

but when that puppeteer-giant's   red heart   let loose
for the open highlands

our school-bell townships   *amalgamated*   went digital
the killdeer's eggs   lost a protector

& the Nihilist Spasm Band pulverized *God Save The Queen*

✕

To listen they lean forward kids do
when you read to them they list
they know how to listen

but adults think of things they have to do
they lean back tick off items on a list
while you read it's to themselves they listen

kids pull the fire out of a word
drawing its heat up into themselves
by magic like a cheroot above an oil lamp used to

but adults have been burnt by words
they know what not to do have trained themselves
to pulse like neon don't waver the ways they used to

if you have a choice read to kids
without a school board close at hand
to tick off which words have been outlawed

lean in to kids
read a monstrosity like a fire in the hand
a classic that was once outlawed

×

(the alphabet)

I tried to be that funny friend
who always has something interesting to say
& makes a lot of sense   but is also a bit of a wing-nut

my poems had my friends in them
so they'd recognize themselves   where we were   what we did
oh I'd take them somewhere else too

not far enough to scare them   just outside the firelight
into the long grass   then back   but now I only have 26 friends
I give a damn about in a poem

I am Godard's *Weekend*   which I haven't seen but I hear is
full of ruthless accidents among friends
(this tort-costume doesn't come off)

I am the n of a broken h
I am half a friend   an end

×

(Praxia)

Before my daughter was born   I made up this whole legend about her

She would lead a band of women resistance fighters   dressed in furs
they would roar across the tundra   on flame-throwing snowmobiles

Hoda   that was her pre-birth name   Hoda would swoop down
from the far North   sabotage Yankee strong-holds

Force the damn Americans out of Canada

~

When she was 4-months-old   we moved to Greece   & lived on Crete
at first   near Agios Nikolaos

In the 1940s   villagers had been massacred by the occupying Nazis
the cathedral had been partially burned   its orthodox icons darkened
by char

I was there   writing on an old door propped between rocks under a
fig tree   because I admired those people who had fought so intracta-
bly for their island back   in ways my own country never would

On the beach   hidden among reeds   I discovered a German
machine-gun bunker: gunless   of crude cement   built to guard the
harbour   & still there in 1989

I would crawl in   like a young German   & watch the ancient water
through the gun-slot

~

In February even while the African sun glared a downpour & double rainbows along the far ridge of the village

Mornings while we bathed the baby in the sink (in warm rain water from a tank on the roof) our landlady's knock at the hot shuttered window an omelette for us a French fry omelette

Brett Brett but she thought the baby's name was *Bread* so she called her the Greek word for bread ψωμί (psomi)

And *we* thought that our landlady's name Praxia meant Peace but it means Action

~

Lady Brett Ashley in Hemingway's *The Sun Also Rises*

That's who we were thinking of a composite with a snoot-full of problems of her own

We forgot about Brett Hull the hockey player son of Bobby

For years Brett gets teased for having a boy's name for being the young sports star

When she's grown she legally adds an *e* to her first name makes it obviously a young woman's name

~

Twenty years the vigilante snowmobiles have grown fainter

On bad days I struggle to convince myself that by merely living as best we could we did anything to improve anything

But then I remember how when Brette's mom was pregnant with her & working as a counsellor at the Morgentaler Clinic in Toronto

Those rabid Fascists with their foetus-posters would scream atrocities at her

As she rode by   beamingly healthy to term   standing heavily to peddle her purple bicycle through them

~

I played table tennis with Morgentaler

That would make a fine title for a kid's book   *Playing Table Tennis With Morgentaler*

He was very good

~

Also   there was a Sri Lankan woman   on strike at a mushroom farm   in Surrey BC   in the early '80s

By the picket-line   as I held the flashlight in the dark trailer   she wrote on my chapati with a marker

The word for *union* in Urdu   & I ate it

~

I used to say   *Retsina is what the gods drink when they can afford it* that meat-freezer-cold pine tang numbing all doubt

The next right thing that makes no sense

I'd take the bus up the cliff from the beach in the morning while Jane & the baby were still asleep

I'd wait in the shade of the square in Zagora for the bakery to open

The next right thing that makes no sense at the time

I'd stumble down through kiwi terraces into the blinding blue of the Aegean

The day's bread a long hot scar against me

Praying to a swallow of light

~

Sloppiness as libation

Sometimes Brette still gets called *Psomi*

A flower   no I mean one who   unplucked   flows   the *o* as in
holy   not *ouch*

~

When I was 5   asleep on a fold-out couch   my cousin Clint Gordon
16 sleeping there too

I woke up he was in me hurting me from behind I tried to get up
he held me down

if you tell   they'll send you to the bad place

it probably happened to him the same way   about the same
age   maybe even the same words

I wouldn't want to be literary here   but I wasn't awake in my life
until then   not aware of myself as existing

my first *me* is this breach   a pain   the conviction that I am
dirty   *guilty*

words have their smells   they hit home

~

Try to think of the plucked stem as a crick   a creek   *scared*   in
flood   lifted out

a three-leggéd meat-eating horse of a river   contorting   above lots &
concessions

~

Cling to pathetic details: the Alcazar Hotel Vancouver Xmas '79 2nd
floor corner

contemplate foaming drizzle   down onto Pender   *only a ballad
mutters now*

stumbling those final tilted blocks into the bindle-stiff
harbor   *as if thrown / of hork & lard*

my banjo's neck had cracked on the train   I threw a *Bic* as hard as
I could against the wall & its plastic splintered

later I crawled around   drinking from the bottle   hunting
that pen's dark inner tube

O mighty quill   it wrote now   a pin-feather bendy to hold

no go the hotel / no go the song   or the cling-to   the long
memory   gulls above slop near the Sea-View

~

Under what you can get away with   is the better line   what you can't
get away from

between sentimentalism   & misanthropy   is the worse
mistake   writing to please

this fiddle-wind I tinker at squealing like goes   *don't eat &
read   come un-Protestant-ing*

~

I am always half   in love with the early   photos of at least   3
women poets

shame honed to defiant beauty   & often I am right   they have been
abused also

not only women   all of us who were made to   we were
  helpless   we absorbed fault

we who blinded half-truths   excoriated normalcy   told disgust a
  joke

to not end up in a ditch   to not go bonkers   to not become
  abusers   we had to tell

when we finally meet   we are safe dry old white flags   with these
  great eyes

our lettered-halves long sunk deep into the red cork of the page

our thumbed guide-feathers whistling

~

Not *holy*   better say *hardworn-sacred*

For once   for once upon   for once open   opening

again to ask the obvious   *it is early so let me*
how can the world be like this   how can the world be like it is

how can this world be is   how can said world be
how be   I ask you   I go to the bathroom flush & wash my hands
maybe I wet my hair or put in a load of laundry   I can hear

the tub filling   I make coffee   & sit here with it   tepid

as I wield my pen   grey dawn in the yellowing elm   rain begins
hear it   punk-elm leaves (eye-shaped)   hear them

this it is all water
this is how be   this be how be   toilet washer-thud taps coffee-rain
ink-aware   a few vitals & their complicated tributaries

oxygen hydrogen carbon   *vitalibutaries*   how can the next choice/word

be liked   there are days I barely notice I am here   & days
I don't notice anything is here but me   those hells

my laboratory the moment
is accordion-shaped   cluttered   sopping

& not eternal

⁕

To pace a pleasing moiety-line

in my brown fedora at dusk in the rain

as I search by our dock for a red stem   (mint)

~

The raccoons have dug up the turtle eggs
but not tipped over Manny's empty ashes-urn

~

Many before us here wrote wider & wackier

Jean Joan Matt McKay Sliter Al Robb

ornate or silly up these draw-road watersheds
they were the daughters of hockey players

(*stupid chickens / fried egg sandwiches*)

Amy Michael Cohen Finnegan Don Kim

that rubber stamp of Dürer's rhino
came down on volumes of exiled theory-song

even the Dalmatian wore a wife-beater t-shirt

Murray Dorothy Wallace Stan Havelock

sunken log barns incubated early styles
lots severed dams imploded sap rang

originals & imitations played euchre

~

Despite poison ivy gnat swarms

deer flies algae bloom zebra mussels
dial-up the OPP firing range

increased traffic on Murphy's Pt Rd

we flaunt a near-town bulk foods happiness
after those difficult city years / ripping money

& kicking the cobbler's bench over

~

Tenebrous   virid   spear

a hint   wild yet / this inextricable quickening

far from   & almost where   I was shown
it could be

×

The Philadelphia Wireman   was probably a woman

a black woman   the neighbourhood
a strong woman   twisting all that wire

an angry woman   twisting all that wire into 1200 scribble-totems

around bits of garbage   she was probably poor
cheap rooms on those streets

she was probably diagnosed *obsessive*

but you & I know better   who say she was *determined*
(wild with the call)   survival driving her right round the bend

the repeated circular motion   a comfort

these her detritus-blows   *work with what is available*
these her fists   found thrown-out beside a dumpster

undelivered from her materials   unredeemed

by a gallery's brightness   no man would love   (you think?)
an empty cigarette pack   like an unborn child

of the revolution   & swaddle it   & swaddle it

in the plumbing of light   an anonymous   poor   strong   angry
black   woman   artist from Philadelphia   spread the word

doelwncoidjtoeifmm6jx   we're not done for

×

A book in its folios is akin to firewood in its split & stacked cords

Blake knows the tree / Whitman knows the tree / bill bissett knows the
tree

I know wet turmoil pidgin'd & the fresh refrain-smell of sawdust

~

A vague grey-wash in the swamp's least twigs

after I have confirmed my ticket I'll have some scrambled eggs
at the diner across the trestle & study again the photos of the old trains

to describe what one does in the early morning always feels like dying
doesn't it

~

I have lived in my body like a drifter
who   cutting across open country   goes to sleep in a barn one night

he wakes up   the barn is on fire   flames everywhere
he can't remember who he is   or where he is

no one watching the barn burn knows who he is either
or how he got there   when he   on fire   comes riding out of the fire

on Abigail   Old Doc's burning white mare

~

Again   with home-made choke-cherry ink   to say the impasse
      the mummified aim

how the dark depth of the standing corn moves as a staggered current
through the rows apace with us as we drive past

under the bond / the carbon   under the carbon / a relentless
      desultory   cross-hatching

✕

Error is Character

Rhythm is Knowledge

Clarity is not pure   it's intricate

×

Again each second the pulse
try to not return unused

us all a strum a face-chord as if soil as if solid

but it's hustings are gushy it's sold
each second the pulse again

try to not return unused

we have heard *us all* dump bodies over ledges into pits before
didn't you once have this falling sickness memorized

the pulse again each second

try to not return unused
stateless the step declares a one foot nationality

an end-stop is a burrow entrance

again each second the pulse
try to not return unused

⁂

Light entered my black song

its banner read *understanding*

I followed it & found atrocity everywhere

~

I have the dates & details wrong   I refuse to understand

I trust my tin-ear / this blind stupid hand gropes

×

(bluegrass)

Arcus / archival / adjectival

a man walks through half of the sun
over fallow land   toward warm windows

each step he takes   makes the earth boom

like a   *like a*   slapped   wash-tub base
around him   & outward   in widening circles

animals scatter   at breakneck   & breakdown speed

their spasms   *covey*   *burrow*   *pod*   *& hoof*

lean in   to one mullein   Aaron's Rod
& are field-recorded   as hectic tin plinks

praised be   *this high-righteous*   *voyage-scraping*

in a log cabin   up Sourdough Mountain   Irene
her pinafore   strumming   fireplace light   an open G

rises   as now   her man stumps in   dragging a fiddle

he has shot for supper   it is tuned high   up near A-flat minor
to harmonize   with the wind   Mariah

revisere / revivere / revere

×

I am roaming the streets
in search of words
to be read at my funeral

I could write them
but what would that prove

if I can find them
out here among panicking strangers

I will have proven
what I set out to prove

I can stop speaking
& go right on speaking

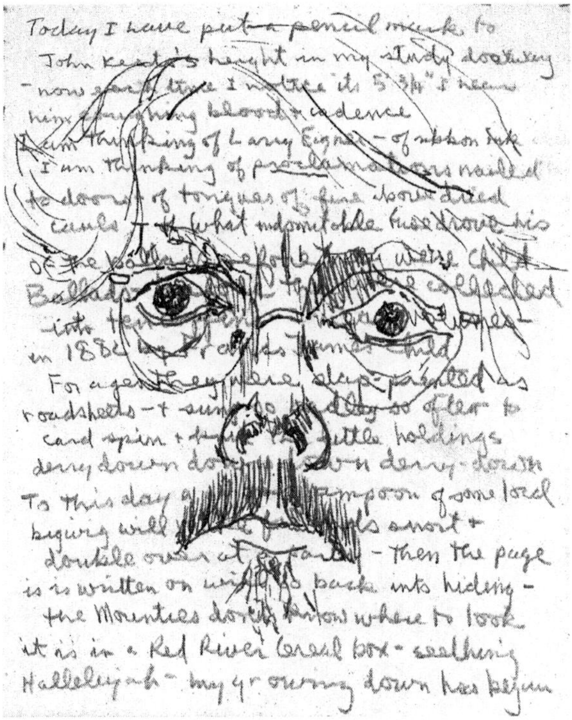
Today I have put a pencil mark to
I am thinking of proclamations nailed
the Mounties don't know where to look
it is in a Red River bread box - seething
Hallelujah - my growing down has begun

Afterword

To See It All & Not Be Weary

I intend to be uncritical   welcoming   accepting

But I need what my poems need   & my poems find out what they need
by identifying what threatens them

What threatens my poems is the urban amalgamation of Voice

What I work to stay clear of   & almost do   is irony

~

I intend to get more generous   deeper & wider

What alternatives others try should be only interesting or disappointing
no threat

I proclaim my hunches about my process   to keep *the mule* of the line
moving   in circles

Now that's a rural image for you   but as easily say   *the lawn mower*

~

Irony   *an inner meaning for a privileged few*

Opposite of that expressed   sarcasm or ridicule

To dissemble   to mock the promise of things & events

Dissemble   *to simulate knowledge or feeling   a guise of ignorance   fake
innocence*

~

Finding   & losing-by-defining   the owl pellet of self

My next line   that it may sing in a way I respect   that is respectful
will be counter to irony

Against the merely weird   opposite to fake feeling

Creatured

~

I find all useful music true

In the measurement sense *true*   & as musical delight

Useful   energy-generating & energy-aiming   humanely

Defining *poetic delight* as   spontaneous pleasure achieved from function-generated arrangements

Out of function comes form

All humanely energy-aiming music I find to be measure & pleasure

The needed music   un-preplanned forms

Defining *humane* as   well   *humane*

~

Which includes   James Hillman reminds us   *to save*   *by remembering the unforgivable*

~

When we say *ironically* in conversation now   we mean little more than *weird*

That what is expressed works two ways   or sets up a passing contrast

But I have heard   *I bow in respect & shame*   that often in the death camps   the last vestige of humanity   was   is   irony

To dissemble in the head when all dignity & hope are crushed

Irony   at its root   then   a survival tool

Yet in its furthest twigs & blossoms   irony can smell of contempt for humanity

Or at least indifference   a flea-focus   *whatever*

~

Against fake innocence & irony

I align myself with what Forrest Gander calls *a rigorous attention to patterning*

To love a poem that risks spelling-it-out & making-it-sing   *unique-ishly* at once

Unique-ish   unsuccumbing to ready ruts   the givens   tropes high tropes low

To love a poem in which *sincerity*   is a devotion to sound & etymology not a sincerity-costume

Patterning   as in layers & proliferation   not textbook patterns the versifiers call form

To love   & aim for   disorienting poems   uninfected by that old bugaboo   *meaning*

No one is eating a plowman's lunch here   no one is talking *definitive*

We are choking on   & coughing up   that elusive owl pellet   slur of little bones from so much reading   self-self

One *wherewithal*   making some noise   *scrawk*

~

One scrawk   yes   yet in *polis*

Only one at a time can write in all these voices   only in our sense of the together gathering of others can we compose ourselves as a single one writing Robert Duncan

One scrawk   yes   yet   *out of*   polis

~

In defense of irony   Mark Kingwall says

The ironist   working in the caesura between seeming & sense   looks insincere but is actually earnest

The bullshit artist   mimicking sincere unction   in fact dissembles

The latter is the enemy of truth   not the former

OK but I have sat through too many poetry readings where a line-break between *peanut*

And   *butter*   has been paused-for   & held

As if the second word   dropped to the next line   were a holy revelation   *butter*

Lyric poets   workshop poets   are the furthest thing from bullshit artists they are trained to venerate niggles of sincerity

Earnestness   squeezed hard enough   or brought to bear on things too small   becomes laughable   a joke   a lie

Now *a satirist*   Rabelais or Paul Hébert   is not an ironist or a bullshit artist   but ultimately a celebrator   an over-doer

Remember that scene in *Night at the Opera*   everyone crowding into the little state-room on the ship

Is my Aunt Minny here   No but you'll probably find someone just as good

Definition & interpretation being different things also   neither objective

Hooray for Groucho   hooray for Chaplin   hooray for Buster Keaton   their populism

In contrast   *in irony*   hear the sneer   in defense of Truth

Yet as the canoe goes over the falls   and flies straight   aloft by one open umbrella

Truth   capital T   is revealed as irrelevant to   lower-case t truth

Which is a complicated ardent mess   at the lip of discovering   itself oddly *pure!*

~

The core of the intent of a lyric line   if it pleases me   is revelation & transformation

Otherwise it lies   is   to my mind   showing-off   demonstrating how smart its author is   or sensitive   manipulating the reader

Often this involves the use of irony

Such a line I call jingo-ism

~

The poem is free to be inarticulate   even to stutter   Peter Quartermain

I align myself with a slipping of the tongue   communication physically burbled

Hunger in the faltering   play ruddered

The *has-to-be-said*   the urge to ur-

~

Out of function comes form

Then the poem will have no form if it has no function

In Whitman or D H Lawrence or Phyllis Webb   the lyric's function is to follow its own urge   outward & inward at once

To measure the first person pronoun's *digit* against a wide horizon of pleasure & grief

Endlessly rocking   so little matters   if there is agitation there is cause

Then function is urge-to-form / & form's best disguise   metamorphoses

Mangrove   pansy or nettle   a tossed white blouse the only word in the dark room

~

Inside the poem   in making the poem   pattern meets risk

If I don't avoid that meeting   by trite metaphor   or the easiest rhyme or bored wordplay to no end

Or by falling back in fear or nostalgia upon set forms   upon imitation

If my next line does not sleep on a mirror

My language may take on a complicating mortal ballast

I might grow   get better at this   be bettered   Othered

~

By *a rural pen* I also mean to remove myself from easy daily dialogue poems

My poem is based on something you said & is dedicated to you yours is reacting to mine & dedicated to me

Plants that grow on other plants or objects & not from soil itself are called *epiphytes*

They can be exquisite orchids they aren't for me

But what madrigals when the arabesques & the straight-goods run off together

Like the dish & the spoon

~

A poetics driven by sub-articulate need no philosophies only necessities Juan Gelman

I don't like jazzed-up British formalist *faux*-genius nor a big-show attack sound rant any better usually

Except maybe green youth I doubt anything justifies cleverness for the sake of anger & noise for the sake of

Hillman speaks of *a program of animism ensouling the nonhuman a program that would relieve the human of its self-importance*

Fur agile fragile

~

A language clarified *by its eccentricities* Gelman

My emphasis on *clarified* as in Blake's use of a rural pen to *stain* the water *clear*

~

I don't accept diluted Symbolist innocence or arrogance either

Playing dumb or wise with shadows & headlines

Assuming the tone of the witty old soul   *spare me*

Pretending we don't know what we know   is disrespectful   a hidden pitch

~

Irony I hear as   *disrespect for subject*   whether lichen or subway

Using the subject to point at the poet   to play *around* a subject so that the main focus stays on the writer

Speaking ecopoetics   Gander   again   describes what I want instead   though it is terrifying

An *intersubjectivity*

~

I stand in Barrie Nichol's heart's tracks

I follow   less flung-heartedly   Steve McCaffery's wide explorations

I am closer to Milton Acorn's rough   embarrassing   passion / than to Irving Layton's classical   embarrassing   passion

I *relish* George Stanley   his voice one long slow mulling of the restless city   his *Vancouver: A Poem*

The body alone on the crowded bus   his absence of irony a stark meandering wake-up

His poem *Veracruz*   one of the most courageous / outlying lyric poems I know

Add Laurie Duggan   & Merrill Gilfillan   *streets & rivers   rivers & streets*

For every Stein-explorer   there are 10,000 typing away   like cummings

~

I suspect that what I am calling *irony*   is what in the past   *at court* was called *wit*

Sir Philip Sydney   in *An Apology For Poetry* says   *our erected wit maketh us know what perfection is...our infected will keepeth us from reaching unto it*

Erected wit / infected will   Sydney saw the necessity of ambition tempered by awe

Those verbs   *erected / infected*   architecture *vs* disease   installation *vs* compulsion

Erected wit   irony   if alone   is without humility   its rapier presumes to imitate the scythes of the gods

Infected will   if alone   unedited by perspective & empathy   as art   can also be presumptuous   unrelentingly humourless   devoid of humility

~

With   & from   & by   imperfection   singing form   *extrapolate* even if   invented   a shared lot

~

Now *urban* becomes *urbane*   to have seen it all & be weary

Poor rural thousands continue to move   or be as refugees   in / into Metropolis

Their subjects change   tool-less   the line   suffers by committee

The instant absorption of strangeness into the Norm is urban   & against the lyric line

A flattening of eccentricities is urban   against the lyric line

~

I rely on internet access here in the bush too

Maybe there is no *rural*   even in the rural   anymore

Is the language of the rustic   as Wordsworth famously claimed   really closer than that of the city dweller   'to the beautiful & permanent forms of nature'   Marjorie Perloff

No   but the I alone   saying its unpredictable measure-pleasure individuatingly

Is in line with   *the revelation that the lyric is   in each iteration   a movement beyond the threshold of the self*   Stephen Collis

Beyond the threshold of the self   this takes us to   is Earl Birney's *Bushed*

~

Incorporation & desperation have generated our recent misnomering of *individual*

Winner self-promoter go-getter beater-outer of others for a prime-share

I retrogress   my *individual* is a Samaritan loner   self-scrabbler   *filius macrocosmi*   lyric-er

In this instance   a left-handed vegetarian no fish doesn't drink smoke or watch TV is allergic to pets loves Joseph Cornell Susan Howe Aimé Césaire *etc*

Spouting names   generous-inclusive   *hopefully*   yet solo-saying

Out of fear   *always*   of illegitimacy   & in homage

~

Perhaps I want the un-artistic as my best song   *fetishized blundermush*

Clearly I label my pen *rural* these days because I live in the bush

Am trying to write a contradiction   *a naive novus*

I want each snaggled grope to be zinging   quirk-*avant*

Yet lonely as erosion-dirt   teeming-common

~

Give waiting to music   the way you'd give   water to horses   Robert Kelly

The barn of flowers pressed to a jumping ounce   James Reaney

~

To be flawed-gone   utterly   into my only   into *my*   into *only*

Hereby   to take the old pen-route   out of *my*   out of *only*

Toward   the music   of us all   *who-all*

—Ph. Otty Lake. 2012—2015

Notes to Afterword

Juan Gelman, edited and translated by Joan Lindgren, *Unthinkable Tenderness: Selected Poems* (Berkeley: University of California Press, 1997).

James Hillman, *Re-visioning Psychology* (New York: Harper & Row, 1976).

*

Rather than explain, I would complicate, rather than define, I would compound, rather than resolve, I would confirm the enigma.

Remember: the enemy is the literal, and the literal is not the concrete flesh but the negligence of the vision that concrete flesh is a magnificent citadel of metaphors.

Peter Quartermain, *Disjunctive Poetics: From Gertrude Stein and Louis Zukofsky to Susan Howe* (New York: Cambridge University Press, 1992).

Acknowledgements

The selections that comprise this volume are taken from the following publications.

I. Books

The Small Nouns Crying Faith (BookThug, 2013)
Killdeer (BookThug, 2011)
The Little Seamstress (Pedlar Press, 2010)
Ghost Gum, with Erín Moure, Mark Goldstein, Jay MillAr, Angela Carr, and Oana Avasilichioaei (Beautiful Outlaw Press, 2009)
White Porcupine (BookThug, 2007)
An Oak Hunch (Brick Books, 2005)
The Bad Sequence (BookThug, 2004; second edition, 2007)
Trouble Sleeping (Brick Books, 2000)
Hearthedral: A Folk-Hermetic (Brick Books, 1996)
The Unsaid (Brick Books, 1992)
Amanuensis (Brick Books, 1989)
Old Enemy Juice (Quarry, 1988)
Why I Haven't Written (Brick Books, 1985)
A Minor Operation (blewointment press, 1984)
Homes (Black Moss Press, 1980)
Eighteen Poems (Cyanamid, 1973)

II. Chapbooks

My Banjo & Tiny Drawings (Flat Singles Press, 2015)
Essay on Legend (Beautiful Outlaw Press, 2014)
Notes from Gethsemani (Nomados Press, 2014)
X (Thee Hellbox Press, 2013)
A Rural Pen (Apt 9 Press, 2013)
Shikibu Shuffle, with Andrew Burke (above/ground press, 2012)
Verulam (above/ground press, 2009)

Pen Is Les Sons (Beautiful Outlaw Press, 2006)
Eighteen Poems (reprised) (Beautiful Outlaw Press, 2005)
Les Transparents (after René Char) (Flat Singles Press, 2002)
Unison-Light (Flat Singles Press, 1985)
A Writer's Guide to Restaurants (Flat Singles Press, 1981)
The Crucifiction (Flat Singles Press, 1979)

lps Books in the Laurier Poetry Series

Published by Wilfrid Laurier University Press

derek beaulieu	*Please, No More Poetry: The Poetry of derek beaulieu*, edited by Kit Dobson, with an afterword by Lori Emerson • 2013 • xvi + 74 pp. • ISBN 978-1-55458-829-9
Dionne Brand	*Fierce Departures: The Poetry of Dionne Brand*, edited by Leslie C. Sanders, with an afterword by Dionne Brand • 2009 • xvi + 44 pp. • ISBN 978-1-55458-038-5
Di Brandt	*Speaking of Power: The Poetry of Di Brandt*, edited by Tanis MacDonald, with an afterword by Di Brandt • 2006 • xvi + 56 pp. • ISBN 978-0-88920-506-2
Nicole Brossard	*Mobility of Light: The Poetry of Nicole Brossard*, edited by Louise H. Forsyth, with an afterword by Nicole Brossard • 2009 • xxvi + 118 pp. • ISBN 978-1-55458-047-7
George Elliott Clarke	*Blues and Bliss: The Poetry of George Elliott Clarke*, edited by Jon Paul Fiorentino, with an afterword by George Elliott Clarke • 2008 • xviii + 72 pp. • ISBN 978-1-55458-060-6
Dennis Cooley	*By Word of Mouth: The Poetry of Dennis Cooley*, edited by Nicole Markotić, with an afterword by Dennis Cooley • 2007 • xxii + 62 pp. • ISBN 978-1-55458-007-1
Lorna Crozier	*Before the First Word: The Poetry of Lorna Crozier*, edited by Catherine Hunter, with an afterword by Lorna Crozier • 2005 • xviii + 62 pp. • ISBN 978-0-88920-489-8
Christopher Dewdney	*Children of the Outer Dark: The Poetry of Christopher Dewdney*, edited by Karl E. Jirgens, with an afterword by Christopher Dewdney • 2007 • xviii + 60 pp. • ISBN 978-0-88920-515-4
Don Domanski	*Earthly Pages: The Poetry of Don Domanski*, edited by Brian Bartlett, with an afterword by Don Domanski • 2007 • xvi + 62 pp. • ISBN 978-1-55458-008-8
Louis Dudek	*All These Roads: The Poetry of Louis Dudek*, edited by Karis Shearer, with an afterword by Frank Davey • 2008 • xx+ 70 pp. • ISBN 978-1-55458-039-2
Paul Dutton	*Sonosyntactics: Selected and New Poetry by Paul Dutton*, edited by Gary Barwin, with an afterword by Paul Dutton • forthcoming 2015 • ISBN 978-1-77112-132-3
George Fetherling	*Plans Deranged by Time: The Poetry of George Fetherling*, edited by A.F.Moritz, with an afterword by George Fetherling • 2012 • xviii + 64 pp. • ISBN 978-1-55458-631-8

Phil Hall	*Guthrie Clothing: The Poetry of Phil Hall, a Selected Collage* edited by rob mclennan, with an afterword by Phil Hall • 2015 • xvi + 72 pp. • ISBN 978-1-77112-191-0
M. Travis Lane	*The Crisp Day Closing on My Hand: The Poetry of M.Travis Lane*, edited by Jeanette Lynes, with an afterword by M. Travis Lane • 2007 • xvi + 86 pp. • ISBN 978-1-55458-025-5
Tim Lilburn	*Desire Never Leaves: The Poetry of Tim Lilburn*, edited by Alison Calder, with an afterword by Tim Lilburn • 2007 • xiv + 50 pp. • ISBN 978-0-88920-514-7
Eli Mandel	*From Room to Room: The Poetry of Eli Mandel*, edited by Peter Webb, with an afterword by Andrew Stubbs • 2011 • xviii + 66 pp. • ISBN 978-1-55458-255-6
Daphne Marlatt	*Rivering: The Poetry of Daphne Marlatt*, edited by Susan Knutson, with an afterword by Daphne Marlatt • 2014 • xxiv + 72 pp. • ISBN 978-1-77112-038-8
Steve McCaffery	*Verse and Worse: Selected and New Poems of Steve McCaffery 1989–2009*, edited by Darren Wershler, with an afterword by Steve McCaffery • 2010 • xiv + 76 pp. • ISBN 978-1-55458-188-7
Don McKay	*Field Marks: The Poetry of Don McKay*, edited by Méira Cook, with an afterword by Don McKay • 2006 • xxvi + 60 pp. • ISBN 978-0-88920-494-2
Al Purdy	*The More Easily Kept Illusions: The Poetry of Al Purdy*, edited by Robert Budde, with an afterword by Russell Brown • 2006 • xvi + 80 pp. • ISBN 978-0-88920-490-4
F.R. Scott	*Leaving the Shade of the Middle Ground: The Poetry of F.R. Scott*, edited by Laura Moss, with an afterword by George Elliott Clarke • 2011 • xxiv + 72 pp. • ISBN 978-1-55458-367-6
Fred Wah	*The False Laws of Narrative: The Poetry of Fred Wah*, edited by Louis Cabri, with an afterword by Fred Wah • 2009 • xxiv + 78 pp. • ISBN 978-1-555458-046-0
Tom Wayman	*The Order in Which We Do Things: The Poetry of Tom Wayman*, edited by Owen Percy, with an afterword by Tom Wayman • 2014 • xx + 92 pp. • ISBN 978-1-555458-995-1
Jan Zwicky	*Chamber Music: The Poetry of Jan Zwicky*, edited Darren Bifford and Warren Heiti, with a conversation with Jan Zwicky • 2014 • xx + 82 pp. • ISBN 978-1-77112-091-3